St. John Fisher Library

share
your read*

*Tell somebody, post a photo, or give this book away to share what you care about.

find more kids books about

autism, addiction, community, sexual abuse, immigration, empathy, suicide, diversity, climate change, gender, and technology.

akidsbookabout.com

Outro

Too many kids go through life feeling confused about adoption simply because nobody has talked to them about it. So let's talk about it! Take some time to explain what makes adoption so special. Even if you don't think you know someone who's been adopted, chances are, you do! Remember that each adoption story is unique and wanting the best for kids is always at the center. Let's not let any more kids walk through life feeling unseen or like they don't belong simply because they were adopted. Be open and honest, but also listen to what comes up with each kid, especially if they're adopted. You may be surprised by what you learn!

Hopefully, this helps you talk about your own stories and feelings about adoption as well.

We feel pride in adoption because it's part of our families' stories.

Leul:
I want kids who are adopted
to know they're not alone,
and they have a friend in me.

I can relate—and I know
others can too.

Nabil:

Yes, my son Adi is adopted, but he's awesome for so many other reasons too!

He has his own story to tell and adoption is only one part of who he is.

I have a beautiful family.
We have so much fun together
and I'm so happy we have each other

All adoptions have
their own unique story.

My story is mine to tell.

Leul:
Adoption hasn't stopped me
from being myself, it's just
a part of who I am.

Adoption isn't just about blood, or skin, or culture.

It's about the act of love and caring for another human, which is really cool.

Nabil:
Seriously! It really is cool.

For my wife and I,
adoption created a new family,
a new bond, and new love
to last forever.

Adoption is COOL!

Chapter Five

Ask, but don't assume—we don't know everything either!

Remember, these are our families. It's personal for us and we have feelings

It's okay for people to be curious about adoption.

So be curious, but be kind.

Where did you come from?
What happened to his real parents?
Do you still talk to them?
Why did your birth parents
not want you?
Did you ever try to have
kids of your own?
Why do you look different
from your parents?

It can be exhausting
and pretty hurtful to hear
these kinds of questions.

Imagine if you were asked questions like these all the time.

Nabil:
Sometimes people make comments that I don't know how to respond to either.

My family feels normal to me, but I can tell we may seem unusual to others.

Leul:

In the past, kids have spread rumors and bullied me because I'm adopted.

They've tried to make me feel bad about it— like I'm different.

Adoption can feel lonely as if you are the only one, but kids are adopted all over the world all the time, you just might not know it!

Others can be curious about adoption.

Chapter Four

There are so many things that make families who have adopted really awesome and unique.

There's no way we could mention them all here, but the list goes

on, and on, and on, and on.....

Leul:
Sometimes you might
have siblings who were also
adopted, like my sister.

Other times you get
new siblings that weren't
adopted, like my little brother!

Kids are adopted at different ages and of all genders.

Kids are also adopted into different types of families.

Some have a mom and a dad,

some have two moms or two dads,

some may just have one,

or neither

Nabil:
My son was adopted domestically, which is a fancy way of saying he was born in the same country we live in.

But even though he was born in the United States, we also are a multiracial family, and that's just us!

Leul:
I was born in another country, which meant my adoption happened internationally.

My family is multiracial, which means we don't all have the same skin color.

When I'm out and about, some people don't get why I look different from my siblings or parents, but that's just us!

No two families ever really look alike—adoption is no different.

Families of adoption are special.

Chapter Three

Adoption is not an easy choice,
but it is a choice made with...

But I know
my birth family
and my family
who adopted me
all love me.

Leul:

My parents adopted me because my birth family made a very difficult choice.

They thought adoption would allow me to have what I needed and would give me more opportunities to grow in a healthy way.

This was really hard.

Kids usually don't get a choice when it comes to being adopted, that's usually up to the grownups, but it does happen sometimes!

Just know, it's never an easy decision to place a kid for adoption, and it's *never* because the kid wasn't loved.

Nabil:

Our son's birth parents chose
to place him for adoption,
and my wife and I chose
to adopt him.

We choose to raise him
and love him forever,
no matter what,
he's our son.

Adoption is a choice.

Chapter Two

and they're **All** special.

We told you!

There really are
so many different kinds
of adoptions...

Nabil:
My wife and I talk
to our son's birth mother regularly
and want her to be a part
of his life forever.

With some adoptions,
kids and birth parents*
aren't able to see each other.

This can feel difficult or sad,
while other times, it might not
seem like that big of a deal.

*birth parents are the people that gave birth to you.

Leul:

I was adopted after
living in a care home.

But even after being adopted,
I still have contact with my
birth mother.

We share pictures and
stories with her often.

Some kids are adopted by other family members or by stepparents.

Other kids may be adopted after living in foster care.

Other times, kids are much older when they're adopted, which can take some time for the kids and their new families to get used to.

When a kid is adopted, they have a new parent or parents.

Those parents are there to help them learn the things they need to know for the rest of their lives and take care of them.

Nabil: Sometimes kids are adopted when they're babies, like my son Adi.

Adoption doesn't always look the same.

There are different kinds of adoptions.

Chapter One

Today,
we want to talk to you
about adoption because
it's something that's close
to us and our families.

There's a lot to know about it,
and it looks a little bit different
for every family, but we want to
help you understand it.

Adi is just like
any other toddler.

He loves to play with toys
and is always learning.

Now he's 2 years old
and we live in Oregon.

My son Adi was born
in Chicago, Illinois.

My wife and I **adopted** him
when he was just born.

Hi, my
name is

Nabil.

Now, I'm 14 years old and live in Oregon.

I'm just like any other kid. I love martial arts, music, and movies.

I'm Black
and was adopted
by white parents.

I was born in
Addis Ababa, Ethiopia.

When I was 2 years old,
I was placed for **adoption**.

Hi, my
name is

Leul.

Intro

All families have their own story, and for some families, adoption is part of that story. It can seem difficult to talk about because there are many emotions surrounding adoption, but when kids talk about adoption, they just want to know the truth. So take it slow and keep the conversation going!

Kids will experience a wide range of feelings and emotions about adoption. At times they may see it as a special and beautiful way for families to come together. Other times they may share feelings of sadness or loss. Those are all normal feelings, and chances are kids will bounce back and forth between them. But the cool part is that you (yes, you!) as the grownup get to help them understand those feelings.

So grownups—you've got this! Help the special kids in your life understand adoption through our story and get ready for a lot of questions!

Leul: In loving memory of my birth great-grandmother.

Nabil: To Courtney, Adi, and Ammu—forever family.

a kids book about™

A Kids Book About books are available online:
www.akidsbookabout.com

To share your stories, ask questions, or inquire about bulk
purchases (schools, libraries, and nonprofits), please use
the following email address:

hello@akidsbookabout.com

ISBN: 978-1-951253-69-1

Designed by Rick DeLucco
Edited by Denise Morales Soto

a kids book about

Adoption

by Leul Gurske & Nabil Zerizef

better together*

*This book is best read together, grownup and kid.